# Blue Whales

## Nature's Biggest Mammal

Taylor Fenmore

Lerner Publications ◆ Minneapolis

Lerner Publications Company
An imprint of Lerner Publishing Group, Inc.
241 First Avenue North
Minneapolis, MN 55401 USA

For reading levels and more information, look up this title at www.lernerbooks.com.

Main body text set in Billy Infant Regular. Typeface provided by SparkType.

**Editor:** Brianna Kaiser **Photo Editor:** Annie Zheng
**Lerner team:** Sue Marquis

**Library of Congress Cataloging-in-Publication Data**

Names: Fenmore, Taylor, author.
Title: Blue whales : nature's biggest mammal / Taylor Fenmore.
Description: Minneapolis : Lerner Publications, [2024] | Series: Lightning Bolt books - nature's most massive animals | Includes bibliographical references and index. | Audience: Ages 6-9 | Audience: Grades 2-3 | Summary: "What are the largest mammals on Earth? Blue whales! Readers will discover how these whales raise their young, what they eat to grow so big, where they live, and more in this engaging text"— Provided by publisher.
Identifiers: LCCN 2023005512 (print) | LCCN 2023005513 (ebook) | ISBN 9798765608395 (library binding) | ISBN 9798765615300 (epub)
Subjects: LCSH: Blue whale—Juvenile literature. | BISAC: JUVENILE NONFICTION / Animals / Marine Life
Classification: LCC QL737.C424 F46 2024 (print) | LCC QL737.C424 (ebook) | DDC 599.5/248—dc23/eng/20230206

LC record available at https://lccn.loc.gov/2023005512
LC ebook record available at https://lccn.loc.gov/2023005513

Manufactured in the United States of America
1-1009284-51493-4/5/2023

# Table of Contents

# Meet the Blue Whale

A blue whale breaches. It exhales from the blowholes on top of its head. Then it inhales and dives back underwater.

**Blue whales are the largest mammals on Earth.** They can grow over 100 feet (30 m) long and weigh up to 200 tons (181 *t*).

# Mealtime

Baby blue whales, or calves, are huge! They weigh up to 3 tons (2.7 t) and are 25 feet (7.6 m) long at birth.

Even though calves are smaller than their parents, calves are still very large.

Calves nurse from their mom. The milk helps them grow. **They gain over 200 pounds (91 kg) a day.**

At about six months old, blue whales start eating krill. Adults eat up to forty million krill every day.

Krill are small animals that are similar to shrimp.

Blue whales have fringed plates called baleen in their mouths. To eat, their tongues push out water through the baleen and swallow krill.

# Strong Swimmers

Blue whales look blue underwater but grayer on the ocean's surface. They have yellow bellies from the millions of tiny animals that live on them.

A blue whale breathing through its blowholes

**They live in every ocean but the Arctic.** Some whales stay in one spot all year. Others move to cooler waters in summer and warmer waters in winter.

Blue whales have two tail fins called flukes, a dorsal fin, and two flippers. Their fins and flippers help them swim.

Blue whales breathe through their two blowholes when they are at the ocean's surface. A special flap covers the holes when they are underwater.

# Long Lives

Blue whales usually live alone or in pairs. Sometimes they live in small groups that eat and travel together.

A blue whale mother and calf

They communicate with sounds like groans. Blue whales are one of the loudest animals in the world. They may be able to hear one another from up to 1,000 miles (1,609 km) away.

A mature blue whale

Blue whales are mature at about six to ten years old. Then a female and a male will mate. They will have a calf about every two years.

Young blue whales stay with their mom for about six to eight months. Then they go off on their own.

A blue whale calf swims alongside its mother.

A close-up of a blue whale

Most blue whales live for eighty to ninety years. **The oldest blue whale ever may have been about 110 years old.**

Blue whales have few predators. These giants rule the ocean. They amaze anyone lucky enough to spot them!

A blue whale breaches the surface of the ocean.

# Blue Whale Diagram

# Fun Facts

- Blue whales can swim up to 20 miles (32 km) per hour.
- A blue whale's heart is about the same size as a small car.
- A group of blue whales is called a pod.

## Glossary

**blowhole:** a nostril in the top of the head of certain animals

**breach:** to leap out of the water

**krill:** a small, shrimplike animal

**mammal:** a warm-blooded animal that nurses

**mate:** to pair for breeding

**mature:** fully grown

**nurse:** when an animal drinks milk from its mom

**predator:** an animal that gets food mostly by killing and eating other animals

## Learn More

Britannica Kids: Blue Whale
https://kids.britannica.com/kids/article/blue-whale/599002

Golusky, Jackie. *Whale Sharks: Nature's Biggest Fish*. Minneapolis: Lerner Publications, 2024.

Humphrey, Natalie. *Blue Whale: Massive Mammal*. Buffalo: PowerKids, 2024.

Kiddle: Blue Whale Facts for Kids
https://kids.kiddle.co/Blue_whale

Leahy, Eliza. *Blue Whales*. Minneapolis: Jump!, 2024.

*National Geographic Kids*: Blue Whale
https://kids.nationalgeographic.com/animals/mammals/facts/blue-whale

# Index



# Photo Acknowledgments

Image credits: Francois Gohier/VWPics/Alamy Stock Photo, p. 4; Ethan Daniels/Stocktrek Images/Getty Images, p. 5; richcarey/iStock/Getty Images, p. 6; VW Pics/Universal Images Group/Getty Images, p. 7; Somporn Pramong/Shutterstock, p. 8; Doc White/Alamy Stock Photo, pp. 9, 14, 18; SCIEPRO/Science Photo Library/Getty Images, pp. 10, 20; Kirk Hewlett/Alamy Stock Photo, p. 11; Digital Vision/Photodisc/Getty Images, p. 12; Heather Angel/Alamy Stock Photo, p. 13; Michael Nolan/Alamy Stock Photo, p. 15; Andrew Sutton/Shutterstock, p. 16; Mark Carwardine/Alamy Stock Photo, p. 17; Anthony Pierce/Alamy Stock Photo, p. 19.

Cover: Blue Planet Archive/Phillip Colla